Mini
MARVELS

Heather Hammonds

Actual size!

OXFORD

UNIVERSITY PRESS

OXFORD
UNIVERSITY PRESS

Great Clarendon Street, Oxford, OX2 6DP, United Kingdom

Oxford University Press is a department of the University
of Oxford. It furthers the University's objective of excellence
in research, scholarship, and education by publishing
worldwide. Oxford is a registered trade mark of Oxford
University Press in the UK and in certain other countries

British Library Cataloguing in Publication Data
Data available

ISBN: 978-0-19-830808-9

11

Paper used in the production of this book is a natural, recyclable product
made from wood grown in sustainable forests. The manufacturing process
conforms to the environmental regulations of the country of origin.

Printed in Hong Kong by Paramount

Acknowledgements

Series Editor: Nikki Gamble
Cover photo: JOEL SARTORE/National Geographic Creative

Illustrations by Tim Bradford
Designed and typeset by Cristina Neri, Canary Graphic Design

The publishers would like to thank the following for the permission
to reproduce photographs: **p2/3**: Panoramic Images/Getty Images; **p4**: Ern
Mainka/Alamy; **p4/5**: Kevin Elsby/Alamy; **p5**: Barrie Britton/Nature Picture
Library; **p6**: John Cancalosi/Nature Photo Library; **p7**: Mlorenzphotography/
Getty Images; **p8**: Reinhard Dirscherl/Getty Images; **p9**: Reinhard Dirscherl/
Getty Images; **p10**: Panoramic Images/Getty Images; **p11**: Panoramic Images/
Getty Images; **p12**: Merlin D Tutle/Getty Images; **p13**: Steve Downer/ardea.
com; **p14**: Kevin Elsby/Alamy; **p15**: Kevin Elsby/Alamy; **p17**: Gary Lewis/Getty
Images; **p16**: NHPA/photoshot; **p18**: Gary Bell/OceanwideImages.com; **p19**:
Gary Bell/OceanwideImages.com; **p20**: Jean Paul Ferrero/ardea.com; **p21**:
Premaphotos/Alamy; **p24**: Mlorenzphotography/Getty Images

Contents

Mini Marvels

Animals come in all shapes and sizes. Some are huge. Others are so tiny that it is hard to see them.

Tiny animals are found all around the world – in forests, on islands and in the sea.

Many of these tiny creatures hide from bigger creatures that would eat them up. Some hide by living high up in trees and others are just very hard to see!

Let's take a look at some of these amazing little animals. They are mini marvels!

Micro Frog

strawberry poison dart frog

This little **amphibian** lives in tropical rainforests. Its bright colours warn other animals that its skin is very poisonous.

The tiny female frogs lay eggs, which the males help to protect. When **tadpoles** hatch from the eggs, they hitch a ride on their mother's back. She takes the tadpoles to live in a rainforest plant until they become frogs.

cm 1 2 3 4 5 6 7 8 9 10 11 12 13 14 15 16 17

A Seahorse So Small

This amazing pygmy (*say* pig-mee) seahorse is found on **coral reefs** in warm, tropical seas. It looks like the coral, which helps it hide from **predators**.

Many pairs of pygmy seahorses live on one piece of coral. The female seahorse lays eggs. Then the male carries the eggs in a pouch to look after them.

About two weeks later, the eggs hatch. The baby seahorses swim away to find their own coral home.

Mini fact file

Lives Coral reefs, western Pacific Ocean

Eats **Plankton** and tiny sea animals

Size About 2 cm

Actual size!

19
18
17
16
15
14
13
12
11
10
9
8
7
6
5
4
3
2
1
cm

pygmy seahorse

Pygmy Leaf Chameleon

pygmy leaf chameleon

Lives Forest, Madagascar

Eats Tiny insects

Size About 3 cm

Actual size!

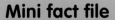

This is one of the smallest chameleons (say ka-mee-lee-onz) in the world. It is so small when it's born that it can fit on a person's fingernail!

During the day, the chameleon hunts for insects on the ground. At night, it rests in the lowest branches of small bushes. It uses its short tail as an extra leg to help it climb.

Like other kinds of chameleons, it can change colour to make it harder to see and to help it hide from predators.

cm 1 2 3 4 5 6 7 8 9 10 11 12 13 14 15 16 17

Micro Bumblebee Bat

The bumblebee bat lives in dark caves in the rainforest. It sleeps during the day.

Just after the sun goes down, this bat zooms out of its cave to hunt insects. It also hunts just before sunrise.

This little night creature makes high-pitched squeaks. Then it listens for the sound to come bouncing back off juicy insects. That's how it finds its **prey**!

Mini fact file

Lives   Myanmar and part of Thailand, South-East Asia

Eats   Insects

Size   About 3 cm

Actual size!

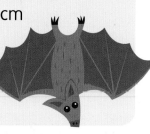

19
18
17
16
15
14
13
12
11
10
9
8
7
6
5
4
3
2
1
cm

bumblebee bat   13

Tiny Bee Hummingbird

bee hummingbird

19
18
17
16
15
14
13
12
11
10
9
8
7
6
5
4
3
2
1
cm

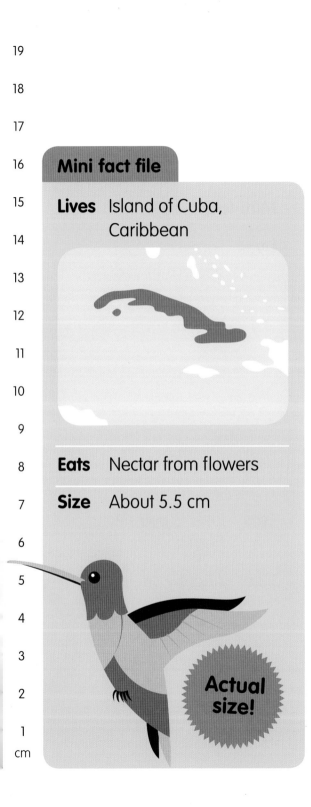

Mini fact file

Lives Island of Cuba, Caribbean

Eats Nectar from flowers

Size About 5.5 cm

Actual size!

The bee hummingbird is so tiny and fast that it's hard to see! It is the smallest bird in the world.

It zips from flower to flower in its tropical **environment**. It eats the sweet **nectar** from tropical flowers.

This mini bird has brightly coloured feathers that help it blend in with the colourful flowers.

Pygmy Possum

This possum is so small that it's no bigger than a mouse! After a long day of sleeping, the cute little micro **mammal** is ready for action.

Using its strong claws and long tail, it scurries around the treetops and hunts for food.

The possum sips sweet nectar and licks **pollen** from forest flowers. Insects are on the menu, too.

Mini fact file

Lives Forest, eastern Australia

Eats Insects and nectar from flowers

Size About 9 cm, with a long thin tail

Actual size!

pygmy possum

cm 1 2 3 4 5 6 7 8 9 10 11 12 13 14 15 16 17

Blue-ringed Octopus

southern blue-ringed octopus

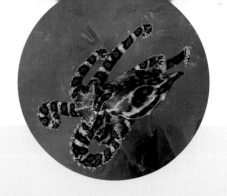

Mini fact file

Lives Oceans of southern Australia

Eats Shellfish such as crabs

Size About 15 cm

Actual size!

The southern blue-ringed octopus lives close to the seashore, around rocks and reefs.

This octopus may be small, but it's one of the most poisonous creatures in the ocean! When it is upset, the blue rings on its body glow brightly. This warns animals to stay away.

This mini sea monster is also a super hunter, using its poison to catch little crabs and other shellfish.

cm 1 2 3 4 5 6 7 8 9 10 11 12 13 14 15 16 17

Flying Dragon

flying dragon

cm 1

Mini fact file

Lives Rainforest,
South-East Asia

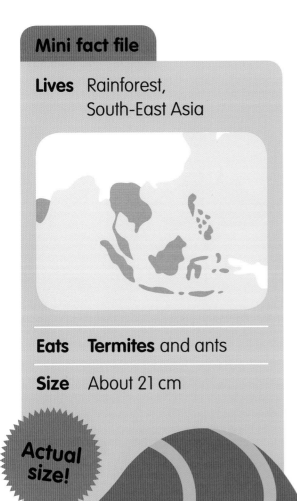

Eats **Termites** and ants

Size About 21 cm

Actual size!

The flying dragon is a tiny lizard. It has very long ribs with special folds of skin between them. These look like wings.

When the lizard spreads its 'wings', it is able to glide from tree to tree in the rainforest. It uses its long tail to steer.

It is not safe for this little lizard to spend much time on the ground. It would soon get eaten by predators. So for most of its life, it stays safely up in the tree branches, gliding around or eating termites and ants.

3 4 5 6 7 8 9 10 11 12 13 14 15 16 17 18 19 20 21

Mini Marvels Around the World

Myanmar and part of Thailand, South-East Asia

Madagascar

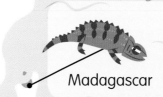

Oceans of southern Australia

Match each name to the correct animal.

strawberry poison dart frog

pygmy seahorse

pygmy leaf chameleon

bumblebee bat

western Pacific Ocean

South-East Asia

eastern Australia

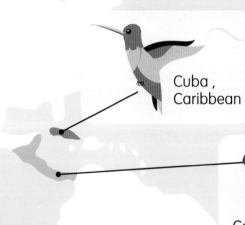

Cuba ,
Caribbean

Central America

bee hummingbird   pygmy possum   southern
                                         blue-ringed octopus   flying dragon

Glossary

amphibian: a cold-blooded animal that lives partly on land and partly in water

coral reefs: ocean areas filled with coral where lots of animals live

environment: everything around a living thing; the natural world that it lives in

mammal: a warm-blooded animal that feeds milk to its young

nectar: a sweet liquid found in the flowers of some plants

plankton: very tiny animals and plants that live in water

pollen: a powder found inside flowers

predators: animals that catch and eat other animals

prey: animals that are hunted and eaten by other animals

reefs: lines of rock or sand near the sea's surface

tadpoles: tiny animals that hatch out of eggs and turn into frogs

termites: small insects that eat wood

Index